~THE~ WILD, WILD WEST

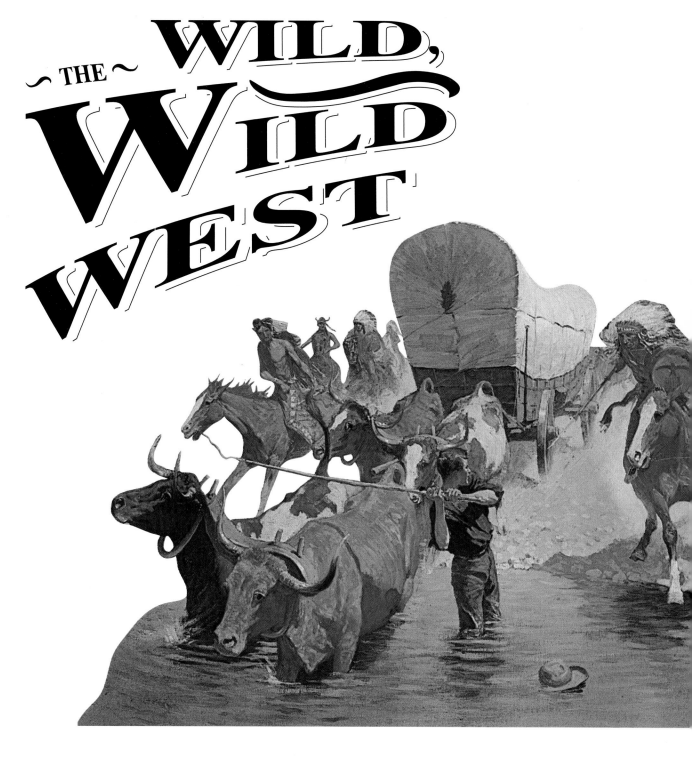

Saviour Pirotta

RSVP
RAINTREE
Steck-Vaughn
PUBLISHERS
The Steck-Vaughn Company

Austin, Texas

THE REMARKABLE WORLD

Published by Raintree Steck-Vaughn Publishers, an imprint of Steck-Vaughn Company

Library of Congress Cataloging-in-Publication Data
Pirotta, Saviour.
The wild, wild west / Saviour Pirotta.
    p.   cm.—(Remarkable world)
Includes bibliographical references and index.
ISBN 0-8172-4536-7
    1. Frontier and pioneer life—West (U.S.)—Juvenile
       literature.
    2. West (U.S.)—History—Juvenile literature.
    I. Title. II. Series.
F596.P57 1996SS
978'.02—dc20   95-49306

Printed in Italy and bound in the United States
1 2 3 4 5 6 7 8 9 0 01 00 99 98 97

Photo acknowledgments
AKG London *front cover* (right), 15r, 17, 18, 22t, 35, 38t, 40tr; Fotomas Index 27, 33; Image Select 8t, 20; Mary Evans Picture Library 5b, 12m, 21b, 24t; Peter Newark's Pictures *front cover* (bl and ml), 6t, 8b, 9 both, 10t, 12b, 13 both, 14, 25 both, 23m, 26 both, 28, 29t, 30, 31, 32r, 34 both, 37t, 38-39, 39t, 40tl, 41, 42, 43, 44 both, 45t; Photri 5t, 21t, 24b, 29b, 40b; Range/Bettmann 6b, 10b, 15l, 16 r, 19, 23b, 32l, 36, 36–37, 37b, 45b; Range/ Calvert 16l; Zefa Pictures 11.
The artwork is by Barbara Loftus.

CONTENTS

THE WILD, WILD WEST

The Wild West of popular imagination reached its peak in the 1870s and 1880s. But its story really began in the 1600s, when various groups of Europeans settled on the East Coast of North America. They cleared the forests, drove away the people who had occupied the land before them, and set up villages and towns, some of which eventually grew to become large cities such as New York and Philadelphia. To the west of this new civilization lay a chain of mountains, the Appalachians, and beyond them, a vast, untamed land stretching all the way to the Pacific Ocean.

This is how North America was divided up between European countries around 1793. The area called Louisiana, which had been given to France in 1800 by Spain, was sold to the United States in 1803 for $15 million. The "Louisiana Purchase" prompted many people to settle west of the Mississippi River.

PACIFIC OCEAN

ROCKY MOUNTAINS

Mississippi River

APPALACHIANS

ATLANTIC OCEAN

☐ Unexplored
☐ Spanish
☐ United States
☐ British
☐ Disputed

The first explorers

About 1787, a handful of pioneers crossed the Appalachians and settled on the land behind them. There they made farmland out of the swamps and forests. Encouraged by their success—and by the American government—more people trekked over the mountains. By 1800, a million settlers were living west of the Appalachians.

In the early nineteenth century, some frontier settlers began to head beyond the Missouri River toward the vast open plains, the Rocky Mountains, and the lush lands on the west coast. Fur traders and explorers had already been there, tracing routes through high mountain passes to the west coast. They were followed by merchants, who organized enormous wagon trains along these routes, leading people across the plains to claim land in Oregon and California.

Jim Bridger **(below)** was a fur trapper, mountain man, and frontiersman.

Members of a religious group called the Mormons escaped prejudice in the East to make a new life for themselves in the West. Pushing handcarts, men, women, and children crossed the desert to found Salt Lake City in Utah. This is a Mormon home on the plains.

Settling the plains

In the 1790s and early 1800s, many cattle farmers, or ranchers, had moved into Texas, where the cattle industry was flourishing. They were followed by the cowboys, the sheep farmers, and the businesspeople who supplied the ranchers with their needs. Before long, the sweeping plains were home to settlers.

This area, far from the coastal cities, is what we now think of as the Wild West. It was a new, largely unexplored country, where Native American peoples roamed in search of buffalo. The plains were wild and inhospitable, scorched by the sun in summer and freezing cold in winter.

A frontier wife collects buffalo chips (dung) for fuel. Life on the frontier about 1800 was very tough. People often felt isolated. They had to be strong-willed to survive.

The Oregon Trail

In 1841, a businessman named John Bidwell organized an expedition to Oregon on the west coast of America. A party of 69 brave men, women, and children traveled in wagons from the town of Independence on the Missouri River. The 1,800-mile journey took them across the wide prairies, through the South Pass in the Rockies, and down the Columbia River toward the Pacific Ocean. During the day, the wagons trundled along at 2 to 3 miles per hour. On a good day they could travel about 24 miles.

The success of the expedition inspired more and more people to emigrate to Oregon. In 1843, about 1,000 settlers had made the journey. By 1845, the numbers had risen to 3,000 a year.

Above The famous covered wagons that trundled across the Great Plains were also known as prairie schooners or Conestoga wagons. They were usually about 13 feet long and only 3 feet wide. The iron wheels gave a very bumpy ride.

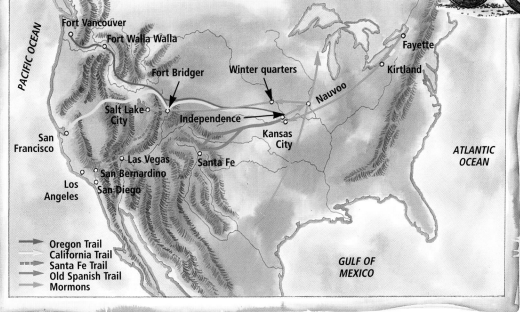

Oregon Trail
California Trail
Santa Fe Trail
Old Spanish Trail
Mormons

Yet it was a place in which strong men and women could stake a claim to their own land and carve out a new life—and maybe even a fortune—for themselves.

It wasn't just the terrain and the climate that made the West wild. Far from the well-ordered communities of the East, the rule of law was often difficult to enforce. Arguments were often settled with gunfights, and lynch mobs sometimes took the law into their own hands and hanged a suspected criminal rather than wait for a visiting judge to hold a trial in court. Cowboys got drunk in town saloons and caused havoc, and crooked medicine show doctors conned people into buying fake cures for all kinds of ailments. Gangs of outlaws robbed banks, stagecoaches, and trains. All the while, the Native American tribes fought a desperate, losing battle to save their lands from being taken by white settlers.

Tales about the Wild West traveled as far as Europe. This illustration from a French magazine published in 1906 shows Native Americans attacking a train belonging to the Southern Pacific Railroad in Arizona.

The lure of gold drew many adventurers to the West. When gold was discovered in California in 1848, more than 100,000 people flocked to its mines immediately. The ones who made it there in 1849 became known as the 49ers. Some had come from places as far away as Europe.

THE COWBOYS

The first cattle to reach America were imported by Spanish settlers in the early sixteenth century. The hot Mexican weather suited the Spanish cattle well, and their numbers grew rapidly. Soon, enormous herds of wild cattle were roaming the land. By the mid-eighteenth century, Spanish cattle farmers had set up profitable ranches in Texas, New Mexico, and Arizona.

News of the wild cattle and the fertile grasslands in Texas reached the settlers coming west over the Appalachians. Many people moved to Texas and started their own ranches. Some created their own herds by capturing wild cattle. Others bought cattle from cowboys who caught and sold the wild bulls and cows. As the cattle industry grew, more people came to the ranches in search of jobs. Many strong, young men were hired as cowboys.

The trail boss was responsible for getting the rancher's cattle—and his cowboys—safely to their destination. He hired trusted men who would obey his orders without argument.

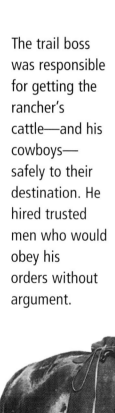

Bronco busters were experts at breaking in wild horses. They were very well paid for their dangerous work, which often meant riding a blindfolded horse. They moved from ranch to ranch, seeking work.

The cowboy's life

Cowboys' duties on a range included rounding up cattle and mending fences. They also branded cows with the rancher's symbol. Before the branding could take place, the cowboys had to capture a cow and hold it down. One cowboy would catch the cow by throwing his lasso around its head. A second cowboy would rope its feet together. The cow was then held to the ground while other cowboys applied a red-hot iron brander to its flanks. Some unscrupulous cowboys were expert at faking symbols or tampering with real ones to make them look different.

Cowboys branded calves with hot iron branders. That way, everyone could tell which cows belonged to which rancher.

American cowboys were very proud of their appearance. They wore trousers with sheepskin or leather chaps to protect their clothes. Some also tied scarves, or bandannas, around their necks. The bandanna was also handy for straining tea, for removing mud from drinking water, and for bandaging wounds.

Cowboys loved listening to stories, especially ghost stories. One tale that made many a spine tingle involved two brothers, named Gil and Zack Spencer. One night in 1890, the brothers were rounding up cattle in Texas when they both set eyes on the same steer.

"I want him," said Zack.

"I want him too," said Gil.

They quarreled, and Zack shot Gil dead. Zack felt so guilty that he branded the steer "Murder" and set it loose. Some time later he killed himself. Soon afterward the steer died, but its ghost was said to haunt the wilderness, frightening people and bringing tragedy to all who saw it.

The cattle drive

After the end of the Civil War in 1865, many Texas soldiers found themselves out of work and short of money. At the same time, the growing population in the north and east of America wanted more beef. So the enterprising Texas ranchers started driving herds to special "cow towns" in the state of Kansas, from where the cattle could be transported by train to other parts of the United States. The great cattle drive became one of the highlights of the cowboy's year.

A group of cowboys in Alaska scare each other with ghost stories. Cowboys liked telling stories, as well as singing and playing card games.

During a trail, food was served from the chuck-wagon. The cook was usually a retired cowboy himself. He served up beans, pork, beef, and black coffee. Although they were surrounded by cows, cowboys rarely had milk in their coffee.

Before the drive could begin, the cattle had to be rounded up. About 20 cowboys would meet the ranch boss early in the morning. After a quick breakfast, the cowboys would fan out across the ranch on ponies and chase the cattle until an enormous herd was assembled. They then lured the young calves that were not yet ready for the market out of the herd.

Once the herd was assembled, the ranch boss hired casual workers to work alongside his cowboys, and a young boy, or "wrangler," to look after the horses. Some wranglers had to look after as many as 150 horses on the trail. Plenty of horses were needed because horses tire quickly in the blistering heat.

A herd of cattle on the trail stop to drink from a river. Trail bosses always made sure they followed a path where the cattle could find water to drink and grass to eat. Hungry cows tended to become slow and nervous.

Trail driving was a very slow process. On a good day, the cattle might travel about 15 miles. At night the herd stopped to rest. While the cattle slept, night watchmen rode among them.

Stampede!

The resting cowboys were very careful not to make too much noise as they ate and prepared to go to sleep. One loud bang from a tin plate could make the whole herd bolt in a stampede. Precious days could be lost in chasing escaped cattle.

Andy Adams, a cowboy who spent 12 years working on trail drives, describes a stampede in his autobiography, *The Log of a Cowboy*. John Officer, another cowboy, was guarding the herd one night when he fell from his horse after the animal had stumbled into a gopher's hole. Officer's cry of pain woke the herd, which then stampeded. Panic ensued as the great herd split into groups, running in all directions. It is impossible to stop stampeding cattle, so the cowboys tried to turn them back.

Sam Colt was the best gunmaker in the Wild West. In 1873, The Colt Company began selling the most famous gun of the time—the Colt .45 single-action army model, also called the "Peacemaker."

Black cowboys

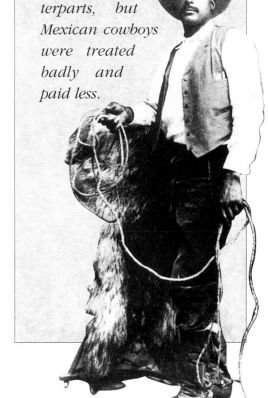

In the early days of ranching, many black slaves looked after the herds in Texas. During the cattle drives, at least a quarter of the cowboys were black, and about a quarter were of Mexican origin. Black cowboys were sometimes treated badly by other cowboys. Sometimes they were not allowed to eat with the rest of group. Many were refused promotion to foreman and were given the worst jobs, like drag riding at the rear of the herd. Ranch owners usually paid black cowboys as much as their white counterparts, but Mexican cowboys were treated badly and paid less.

Shouts of "Stampede!" usually meant a sleepless night for the cowboys. Sometimes they would stop the cattle from bolting by forcing them into a circle. Some stampedes were started by unscrupulous rustlers who would steal some cattle while the cowboys were busy rounding up the herd.

They fired their guns in front of the leading bulls' faces, hoping to make them run back toward the main herd. They also tried to prevent the groups from breaking into smaller ones. At one point, Adams was caught in the middle of a fleeing herd. Closing his eyes, he held on to the reins and hoped he would not be trampled to death. The running cattle ripped his clothes, completely tearing off the sleeve of his shirt. His face was covered in thorns. When the sun came up, the cowboys got lost in the morning mist. It took a long time to get the vast herd back together again. By the time they succeeded, the cowboys were exhausted.

Most trail drives lasted at least three months. When a drive was over, the cowboys made up for all their hard work in the saloons of the cow towns, drinking, gambling, and dancing all day and all night. The partying often led to arguments and violence.

Paid off and out of work

After the drive, many cowboys lost their jobs. Most survived by hunting wild animals and doing odd jobs, such as chopping firewood. Trusted cowboys were sometimes allowed to stay on at their ranches. They weren't paid any money, but they got free meals and a roof over their heads at night.

Cowgirls in the rodeo

Since women were expected to look after the house and family, few of them could go on the long trail drives or work on far-flung ranges. Many women, however, learned the same skills as their male counterparts.

Prairie Rose Henderson was an expert bronco rider who used to wear a brightly colored skirt. She was so popular with the audience that many other rodeo shows felt they also had to hire a cowgirl. One of the most legendary of these cowgirls was Lucille Mulhall, who could catch eight horses at a time with one throw of her lasso. She could also rope coyotes. Buffalo Bill considered Lucille to be the best cowgirl in the world.

Perhaps the most famous cowgirl of them all was Martha Jane Cannary, more popularly known as Calamity Jane. Martha used to wear buckskin trousers and cowboy hats. She spent a lot of time in dance halls drinking and fighting with the men.

Left Calamity Jane's fondness for guns was legendary.

Right A rodeo cowgirl in 1910, complete with her lasso and gun

LIFE IN A WESTERN TOWN

As settlers and pioneers pushed the frontier ever westward, towns sprang up along the main transportation routes. Most frontier towns started off as trading posts surrounded by a few cabins. The trading post was a focus for the local community, where settlers could sell their produce and buy goods imported from the East. Some of the towns flourished and grew rapidly. Others simply faded away in a year or so and became nothing more than ghost towns.

A wagon train reaches a farming community in the 1880s. Most towns in the West began as a group of huts. Some survived and grew into large towns, while others faded away.

Below During its heyday, Bodie was one of the liveliest cow towns in the West. But when business dried up, Bodie became a ghost town.

Long-distance travel in the West

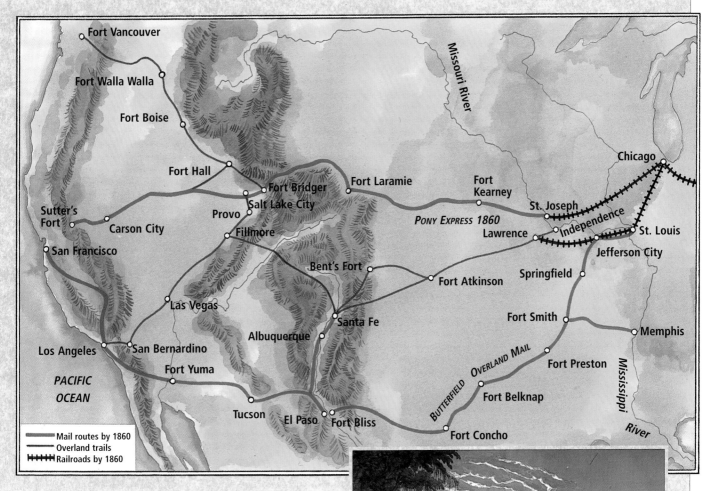

Mail routes by 1860
Overland trails
Railroads by 1860

Fort Vancouver
Fort Walla Walla
Fort Boise
Fort Hall
Fort Bridger
Fort Laramie
Fort Kearney
St. Joseph
Chicago
Sutter's Fort
Provo
Salt Lake City
Pony Express 1860
Independence
St. Louis
Carson City
Fillmore
Lawrence
Jefferson City
San Francisco
Bent's Fort
Fort Atkinson
Springfield
Las Vegas
Santa Fe
Fort Smith
Memphis
Los Angeles
San Bernardino
Albuquerque
Butterfield Overland Mail
Fort Preston
Fort Yuma
Fort Belknap
Mississippi
PACIFIC OCEAN
Tucson
El Paso
Fort Bliss
Fort Concho
River
Missouri River

By 1860, people moving to the West could travel by steamboat or stagecoach—the railroad had only reached the Missouri River. Steamboats (right) carried passengers and goods like sugar and cotton.

Western towns could be reached by stagecoach, by steamboats, and by rail. Steamboat travel began in 1811, when the New Orleans sailed along the Mississippi River from Natchez to New Orleans. The boats carried passengers and goods to be sold in other towns. Many steamboats were like floating palaces, complete with bars and gambling salons. But they could explode very easily and were easy targets for attack by Native Americans. The age of the steamboat ended in the 1870s, when the train took its place.

Stagecoaches outlasted the steamboats by many years. The first transcontinental stage line was known as the Butterfield and was opened in 1858. It went all the way from St. Louis, Missouri, to Tucson, Arizona, then up to San Francisco, a journey of about 3,700 miles. At the height of the Butterfield's popularity, 250 coaches were in use at any one time.

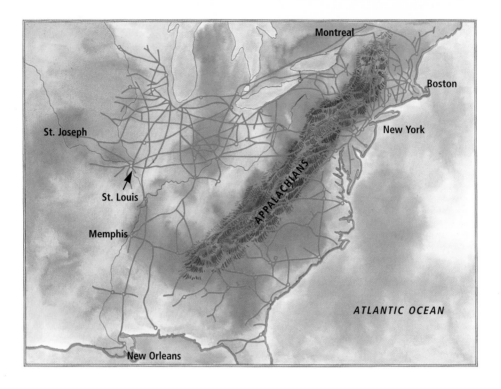

Train tracks from the East Coast to the cities west of the mountains in 1854. Railroads made moving over the Appalachians, which had been the border with unsettled lands to the west, easier and safer.

Building a new town

Settlers' towns were usually built close to transportation routes. The founders of mining towns were not so choosy. They built their towns as close to the mines as possible, even if it meant constructing houses on steep hills. When the mine ran out of minerals, all the workers and their families simply left the town and moved somewhere more promising.

Sometimes, a small group of settlers would get together and set up a small town, hoping to attract residents who would buy their land.

An Overland Mail Company stagecoach hurries toward its destination in California carrying mail, freight, and passengers. It took such coaches some 25 days to reach their destination after leaving St. Louis, Missouri. There were resting stations for the drivers and passengers roughly every 20 miles.

One such place was Omaha, Nebraska. It was founded in 1854 by a committee that included a sheriff, doctors, merchants, and land speculators. The project was a success, and Omaha—named after the local Native American people— became an established city.

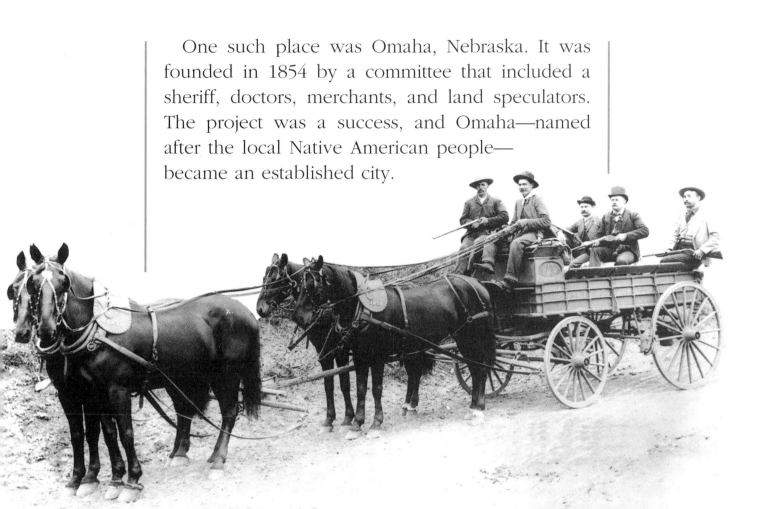

Wells Fargo

At the heart of each town was the express office. Since there was too much mail for the governmental mail to deal with, private delivery companies were set up. The most famous of these was Wells Fargo. It had offices in many towns, where people could mail anything from letters to gold dust. The arrival of the express was eagerly awaited by the inhabitants of any town. Everyone stopped working and rushed to the local store to find out if there was anything in the mail for them.

A Wells Fargo treasure wagon near Deadwood, Arizona. The men are guarding $350 worth of gold bullion.

The Pony Express

On April 3, 1860, Johnny Frey, a slim, young seventeen year old climbed onto a pony in St. Joseph, Missouri. His brand-new saddle had four pockets, each filled with letters wrapped in oilskin to protect them from the weather. As Johnny thundered off, a band played, and steamboats on the Missouri River hooted their horns. Johnny was a rider in a new mail service called the Pony Express.

The idea behind the Pony Express was simple. A group of 80 or so riders—and 500 fast ponies—carried letters between St. Joseph and Sacramento, California. To lessen the load, letters sent by Pony Express had to be written on very thin, lightweight paper. There were 190 stations along the 2,000-mile route. As each rider galloped into a station, another would be

The firm of Russell, Majors, and Waddell who set up the Pony Express required their riders to be young, slim, and willing to risk death daily. Orphans—with no parents to lament their deaths—were preferred. In this picture, a Pony Express rider is being pursued by a Native American.

waiting for him. The riders had only two minutes to exchange their saddles containing the mail before setting off again.

The Pony Express lasted only 18 months. It was killed off by the arrival of the telegraph, which could send messages along wires from one side of the country to the other in a matter of minutes. In its short lifetime, the Pony Express delivered 34,753 letters and parcels, and its young riders became national heroes.

Funny money

A town's main street also contained the bank—usually a branch of one of the big banks in the East. It was often opened as soon as a settlement was established—and closed just as quickly when things went wrong and the people moved on.

Most banks printed their own banknotes and made their own coins. Sometimes there were so many different coins in use that it was easy for crooks to pass counterfeit money.

Daniel Robertson, the Marshal of Ohio, was an expert at catching forgers. In the late 1840s he tracked down an infamous counterfeiting gang led by James Burns and his wife. Robertson and his deputy, D. K. Goodin, chased Burns all the way to a house in Virginia. Hearing the marshal in the front room, Burns tried to escape quietly through the back door, but he walked straight into the arms of a waiting posse.

Wars of words

Another important part of town was the local newspaper office. Frontier people loved newspapers because they made the people feel that their town was permanent and respectable.

Buildings such as these shops on Broadway Street in Round Pond, Oklahoma Territory, had false fronts to make them look more grand than they really were. Adding a false second story was especially popular. Shopkeepers often bought do-it-yourself books that showed them how to construct a building.

General stores like this country store sold everything from food to clothes, tools, and ammunition.

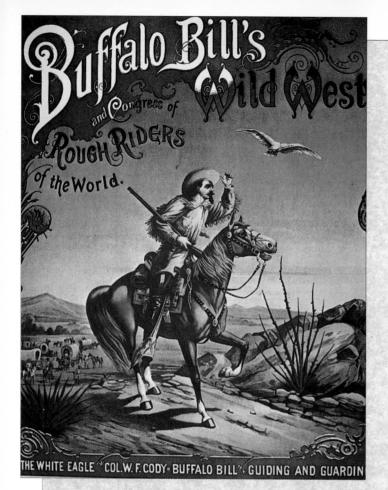

THE WHITE EAGLE "COL. W. F. CODY - BUFFALO BILL" GUIDING AND GUARDIN

Before starting his show, Buffalo Bill had a humbler job—catching buffalo to feed railroad workers.

Buffalo Bill

For years, Buffalo Bill's Wild West Show thrilled audiences in America and Europe. Buffalo Bill (real name William Fredrick Cody) was a famous buffalo hunter who turned to show business. His act included cowboys and Native Americans. The cowboys performed a rope-throwing act called rodeo, which is still a popular entertainment today. The highlight of the Wild West Show was a stagecoach holdup by a posse of criminals.

In 1887, Buffalo Bill and his performers traveled to Great Britain. Their show was a thrilling success and was seen even by Queen Victoria. After the show, the royal princes were given a ride in a real stagecoach.

In 1893, Bill's show was excluded from the Chicago World's Fair because there was insufficient space inside the Fair. Bill's partner leased land opposite the Fair and held his own show. It attracted so many people that some thought it was the World's Fair.

Newspaper articles were often very controversial and caused no end of trouble. Writers who applied for a job with the *Territorial Enterprise*, whose most famous writer was the novelist Mark Twain, were not asked whether they could write. The editor wanted to know how good they were with guns. Journalists who wrote troublesome articles were expected to defend their views. Outraged readers sometimes tried to murder or harm the writers. One editor with the *Enterprise* named Wells Drury was attacked by a reader brandishing a bullwhip. Drury shot the man dead.

Preachers and medicine show doctors

Preachers often arrived in town shortly after the newspapers. In the smaller towns, they held their services in shops or private houses. In the larger ones, the residents would erect a church as soon as they finished building their own homes and shops.

The biggest attraction for a town's inhabitants were the medicine show doctors, who were very popular after the 1860s. They were crooks who tricked people into buying fake "medicines." Medicine show doctors were often accompanied by singers or other acts who would attract potential victims. Some of the fake medicines peddled by the con men included Dr. Sherman's Pricklyash Bitters, which were claimed to cure a wide range of ailments, including constipation, heartburn, flatulence, torpid liver, diarrhea, and irregularities of the kidney.

A traveling medicine show doctor peddles a tonic guaranteed to cure all sorts of ailments and diseases. Some clever con men employed singers to attract customers.

A group of people waiting to see a "healer" in Denver are treated to a free lunch. Traveling ministers used all sorts of tricks to raise money for their churches. A few were even known to hold their parishioners at gunpoint until they got a donation.

A group of cowboys hit the local saloon for a night out. Some bars didn't mind cowboys bringing their horses along for a drink but others insisted the animals be left outside.

The lure of the cow towns

Perhaps the most notorious towns in the Wild West were the cow towns, or trail towns—such as Abilene and Dodge City in Kansas—where the cattle were brought for sale. Tired, thirsty, and bored after three months on the trail, the cowboys rode into town at a full gallop, letting their cows run along the streets. After the cattle were penned, the cowboys went out to spend the money they had just earned and to get some excitement. First, they would get a haircut and a shave and buy some new clothes. Then, with pistols hanging on their hips and the spurs shining on their new boots, they charged into the local saloons. Days of drinking, dancing, and gambling followed—along with plenty of gunfights and fistfights—as the cowboys spent their money as quickly as they could.

Abilene was the most notorious of all the cow towns. It had so many saloons, beer gardens, and dance halls that local people called the area "The Devil's Addition." The Alamo Saloon had a bar with brass fixtures and flamboyant paintings.

For many cowboys, a night of drinking in a saloon with a name like Pearl and Old Fruit was the only release from a life of hard work.

Bands played music continuously while the customers gambled at cards with Wild Bill Hickok, the local marshal, who used the saloon as his headquarters.

One day in 1871, Wild Bill accused a man named Phil Coe of cheating at cards. There was a short gunfight in which Coe was killed. Wild Bill also accidentally shot one of his deputies. He was so angry that he chased all the cowboys out of Abilene. The local farmers had also had enough of the wild cowboys. In 1872, they forbade the cattle trails from entering the city. This proved disastrous because cattle ranchers took their business to other towns, and Abilene lost a lot of money. Some of the saloons in Abilene were dismantled and shipped by railroad to other cow towns. That way, the cowboys could enjoy themselves wherever the trails stopped.

Professional card cheats haunted the bars and saloons of the Wild West. Their games often ended in violent quarrels—and sometimes shootouts.

Above The famous marshal James Butler "Wild Bill" Hickok was a scout for the U.S. Army before donning the badge. He was shot dead in Deadwood, Arizona, in 1876 by a criminal named Jack McCall. Wild Bill's loyal followers immediately set up a people's court and sentenced the killer to hang.

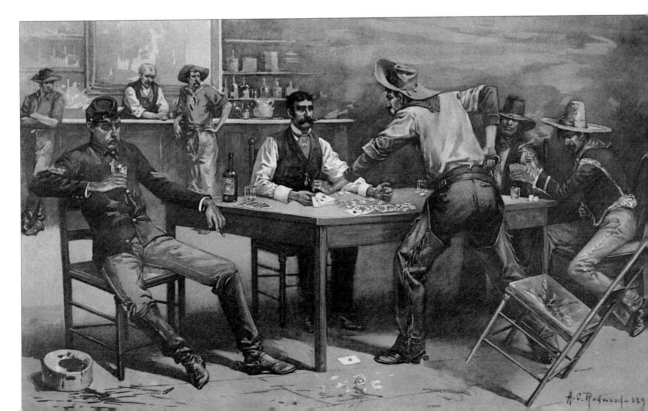

KEEPING LAW AND ORDER IN THE WEST

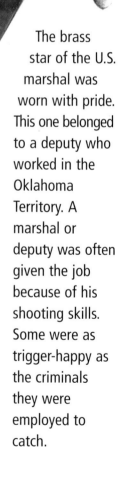

A group of vigilantes ride away after hanging a suspected criminal. Lynch mobs often punished a criminal before the lawmen could get to him. Sometimes they made mistakes and executed the wrong person.

Many Western towns and settlements were a long way from well-organized cities, so they attracted many lawless people who saw a chance to work outside the limit of the law. To protect their law-abiding citizens, many towns elected their own marshals and sheriffs.

The U.S. marshal was responsible for keeping the law in an entire state or territory. Town marshals and their deputies kept the law in their own towns on behalf of the American government. If the mail or a train was held up or if a government official got shot, the marshal would step in. The sheriff and his deputies worked for a town or county. Their job was to protect the local citizens and deal with crime against private homes and businesses. When needed, civilians were called on to help the marshal and sheriff.

Sometimes people formed vigilante groups, or "lynch mobs," to deal with local criminals before the lawmen arrived. An early example of the lynch law dates from 1834, when a band of angry men hanged a gambling cheat in Vicksburg, Mississippi.

The brass star of the U.S. marshal was worn with pride. This one belonged to a deputy who worked in the Oklahoma Territory. A marshal or deputy was often given the job because of his shooting skills. Some were as trigger-happy as the criminals they were employed to catch.

Cattle rustlers raid a Texas herd. Some people tried to start their own ranch by stealing cattle from the big ranchers. Professional rustlers also made a profit from selling stolen cattle.

Marshals and sheriffs in cow towns had the difficult job of dealing with wild cowboys when they got into fights. They also had to deal with cowboys, buffalo hunters, and soldiers who turned to organized crime when they were out of work. In southwestern towns, catching criminals was often very difficult because the villains kept escaping over the border into Mexico.

Jesse James

In the late 1860s, after the Civil War, many ex-soldiers from the losing Confederate army turned to crime. One of the most notorious criminal gangs of the nineteenth century was led by Frank and Jesse James. The James brothers had fought on the Southern side during the Civil War. Afterward, they

Wild women of the West

Lawlessness in the Wild West was by no means confined to men. Belle Starr, a cattle rustler and expert horsewoman, could outshoot any average marshal. She had a string of criminal boyfriends, including Sam Starr—known to the law and the outlaw gangs as Blue Duck—whom she married. Belle raised her son to be a horse thief.

Her temper was famous. One day, while leading a band of horse thieves across a gulch, Belle's new hat blew off in the wind. No one looked as if he was going to retrieve it. An angry Belle pulled out her gun and pointed it at her husband.

"Haven't you got any manners?" she screamed. "Get off that horse and fetch my hat." Blue Duck, of course, obliged right away.

"Cattle Kate" and her business partner, James Averill, stocked their herd in Wyoming with rustled cattle. After defying an order to leave the country, they were hanged by a lynch mob.

were treated as heroes by the people in their hometown, no matter what they did.

In 1866, the James brothers walked into a bank in Liberty, Missouri, pretending they wanted change for a ten-dollar bill. They held up the bank and managed to escape with $60,000 in cash. During their raid they killed an innocent 19-year-old boy. Angry locals formed a vigilante posse and set off after them. They nearly caught up with them on the banks of the Missouri, but the gang had crossed the river and a storm prevented the posse from following.

Once, when her husband lost $2,000 gambling in a Dodge City saloon, Belle said, "Never mind, a pair of six-shooters beats a pair of sixes any time." With that, she marched into the bar, held the gamblers at gunpoint and walked out with $7,000. "Five thousand dollars is for interest," she laughed.

When Belle's gang got caught, she tried to bribe the authorities into letting them escape. But it was no use. Blue Duck was found guilty of murder and sentenced to hang. The resourceful Belle wrote to the president and got his sentence commuted to life imprisonment. Belle came to an untimely end when she was shot dead in 1889.

Other legendary gun-toting women included Big Nose Kate, Minnie the Gambler, Madame Mustache, and Mattie Silk, who were all gamblers with short fuses. Rose Dunn, known by all as the Rose of Cimarron, was an expert horse thief. She terrified all who knew her, even her husband, the infamous outlaw "Bitter Creek" George Newcomb.

Belle Starr liked to think of herself as "The Queen of the Outlaws."

In the next fifteen years, the James gang robbed no fewer than twelve banks, seven trains, and five stagecoaches. The marshals did everything they could to catch the gang, but they never succeeded. Eventually, Jesse was shot in the back by Bob Ford, one of the members of his own gang.

Left Frank and Jesse James (seated) pose for a picture with gang members Cole and Bob Younger.

Frank and Jesse James's gang rob a train belonging to the St. Louis Midland Railroad. The rail company later offered a reward of $25,000 for the capture of Jesse. Another $15,000 was offered for Frank, and the other gang members had a price of $5,000 each on their heads.

Frank turned himself in, but the southern jury considered him a war hero and did not convict him. He lived on his farm until his death at age 82.

Wyatt Earp

The most legendary lawman of the cow towns was Wyatt Earp. Three of his brothers—Virgil, Morgan, and Warren—were also lawmen. Many honest citizens disliked the Earps, who always banded together. But no one could deny that they were brilliant at their job. The criminals hated Wyatt Earp even more. They saw him as a threat to their way of life, and many tried to kill him, both for revenge and for fame.

Before donning the marshal's badge, Wyatt worked as a professional gambler, a buffalo hunter, a stagecoach driver, and a referee in prizefights. In 1875, he was arrested during a fistfight in the cattle town of Wichita, Kansas. Before he could be taken to jail, a gang of cowboys started to rampage through the town. Wyatt offered to help the marshal deal with them. Afterward, he was made deputy marshal.

Later, Wyatt was made marshal of Dodge City, the biggest trail town in Kansas. During the 1870s, half a million cattle passed through it every year. It was also the favorite town of thousands of cowboys. Many infamous people were buried in its Boot Hill cemetery. Wyatt Earp stayed in Dodge City until it was cleaned up in 1879. Then he went to Tombstone, a tough mining town in Arizona where criminals were hanged from telegraph poles.

Wyatt Earp and his brothers shoot it out in 1881 with a bunch of cowboys at the O.K. Corral.

Pat Garrett and Billy the Kid

Billy the Kid became an outlaw at a young age. Legend says that he killed his first man, a blacksmith, at the age of 12, when the man insulted Billy's mother. Fleeing from justice, Billy and a friend went to Mexico and made occasional cattle rustling raids into New Mexico.

In 1878, Billy got caught up in the Lincoln County Range War. This was a feud between a big cattle rancher named J. S. Chisum and his rival, Major Murphy, a shop owner who had a small ranch next to Chisum's and who led a band of cattle rustlers. Murphy was a powerful man in the town because he appointed the local sheriff.

The famous sheriff Pat Garrett was an old friend of Billy the Kid. That didn't stop him from shooting the wanted criminal.

Two of Chisum's friends—John Tunstall, an English rancher, and a lawyer named McSweeney—opened a general store and took away a lot of Murphy's trade. When Chisum opened a bank in the store, Murphy decided it was time to act. Meanwhile, Billy the Kid turned up at Tunstall's ranch looking for work and was hired on the spot. A few months later, a posse organized by Murphy killed Tunstall and stole his cattle. Billy swore to avenge Tunstall's death. The violent feud continued for months, with both sides killing members of the opposite gang. Billy refused to stop fighting, even after the range war was officially ended. He formed his own gang of ruthless men and scoured the ranges, killing cattle rustlers and stirring up battles.

People liked Billy despite his violence, and they helped him when he needed food and information.

Billy the Kid's image as a rather helpless boy helped to make him a national hero, despite the many acts of violence he committed.

Finally, the authorities hired Pat Garrett as sheriff and told him to hunt down the Kid. Garrett tracked him down to a hut in Stinking Spring and arrested him. Billy was tried in court and sentenced to hang. The night before his execution, Billy escaped. Pat Garrett went after him again. He chased Billy to Fort Sumner and shot him dead.

THE FATE OF THE NATIVE AMERICANS

In the early 1800s, there were about 360,000 Native Americans living west of the Mississippi River. Some lived in California and the northwest. Many inhabited the south and high plains. The plains-dwellers lived off the great buffalo herds, which they thought would never run out.

Broken promises

When white settlers migrated across Native American territory to Oregon and California in the 1840s and 1850s, they were met with only occasional resistance from Native Americans. The

Peikan Native Americans set up camp. The Native Americans tamed the wild descendants of horses introduced to the country by Spanish conquistadors in the sixteenth century.

American government had promised them that the land to the west of the Missouri River would be theirs forever. But the settlers' forts and towns soon began to grow bigger. The government kept breaking its promises by allowing Europeans to settle on Native American territory. Some Native Americans started to attack settlers and to raid forts, towns, stagecoaches, steamboats and, later, railroad trains.

In 1851, government officials met with Native American chiefs at Fort Laramie in Wyoming to sign the treaty of Horse Creek. More than 10,000 Native Americans turned up for the great meeting. They agreed to let the settlers pass safely through their land and to build forts and roads. In return, they were guaranteed various territories, which the government promised would never be touched. Another treaty giving the same guarantees was signed two years later by Native Americans who had not been at Fort Laramie.

Fort Laramie was at the heart of the Wild West's history. It was first used by fur traders. Pioneers on their their way to Oregon stopped there to rest. Later it became an important out-post of the U.S. Army.

The Native Americans were alarmed when the trickle of white people crossing the plains turned into a never-ending flood. They began attacking the forts that had been built by the U.S. Army.

A Sioux warrior injures a cow owned by a Mormon settler. The incident was to escalate into a major battle with the U.S. Army, one of whose officers mistakenly considered all Sioux and Native Americans to be cowards. The U.S. soldiers were annihilated. The Commissioner for Indian Affairs later admitted that the army had attacked the Sioux without permission.

Grattan's Massacre

In 1854, a major fight broke out between the Teton Sioux and officers of the American army. It began when a Sioux hunter shot a sick cow belonging to a Mormon settler. The settler reported the incident to the army in Fort Laramie. An arrogant officer named J. L. Grattan was ordered to arrest the Sioux. He rode out with 29 soldiers to deal with them. The two sides met in the North Platte Valley. One of the Native American chiefs, Conquering Bear, offered to pay for the cow with horses. But Grattan and his men were in no mood to negotiate. Someone fired a shot, and before Conquering Bear could calm everyone down the officers had opened fire. In the battle that followed, Conquering Bear was badly wounded, and Grattan and all his men were killed.

Red Cloud's war

After what was called "Grattan's Massacre," hostilities between the Native Americans and the settlers continued for 30 years. In June 1866, the American government sent Colonel Carrington and General Sherman to organize another big peace meeting with Native Americans. The Native Americans attended, even though the government had not kept its previous promises. General Sherman asked for permission to open a road along the Bozeman Trail, which joined the Platte River with the Montana gold mines, and to fortify it with three forts. This was against the terms of a previous treaty. Red Cloud, a Sioux warrior, walked out of the meeting when he realized that the army would build the forts whether or not he accepted. The other chiefs followed Red Cloud. They warned the officers that they would do all they could to stop the building of the forts and the road.

Despite the Native Americans' treaties—and the attacks they carried out on the soldiers and builders—by the end of October 1866 Fort Phil Kearney was ready. On December 6, Red Cloud led over 2,000 Apaches, Arapahos, and Cheyennes toward the fort. Many of them hid in the foothills around it while a number of Sioux attacked a group

Chief Red Cloud was an Oglala Sioux. When the Army trespassed on land considered to be Sioux territory, Red Cloud told Colonel Henry Carrington, "You steal the country before the Red Man has a chance to say yes or no."

Custer's famous Last Stand lasted only half an hour. In that time, Custer and his 264 soldiers were all killed.

36

Crazy Horse and Custer

Above A portrait of Crazy Horse, painted by artist Robert Lindneux

As a child, Crazy Horse was considered to be extremely gifted, though rather strange. He was given his name after having a dream in which he saw a mad horse. The elders of his tribe believed the dream meant that the boy would help rid their country of white people. Crazy Horse's chance to fulfill this prophecy came in the 1870s.

In 1871, work started on preparing the land around the Black Hills in Dakota Territory for laying railroad tracks. The Sioux were angry. Their leaders—Sitting Bull, Crazy Horse, and Red Cloud—reminded the whites that the Black Hills were sacred to them. The American government, which they called The Great White Father, had promised to leave the Hills alone in a treaty signed in 1868. The work continued nonetheless, and fighting flared up between the Sioux and a detachment of the U.S. Army led by Lieutenant General George Custer.

In 1874, gold was discovered in the Black Hills. White men rushed to the spot in search of their fortunes. The Sioux were outraged. The U.S. government offered to buy the land for six million dollars. The Native Americans would not sell; the Black Hills belonged to them. So both sides were drawn into war. During a major offensive in June 1876, Custer led his 7th Cavalry to a Sioux village. He was attacked by Crazy Horse's men and by the warriors of another chief, Gall. Custer and all his men were killed.

That night the Native Americans held a scalp dance around the fire. They had beaten the white man. But Custer's Last Stand, as the victory came to be known, was the Native Americans' last victory. They were hounded by the army until they had to give up. As he surrendered, Chief Crazy Horse shook his left hand with his captor, Lieutenant Clark. He said, "Friend, I shake with this hand because my heart is on this side. I want this peace to last forever."

Custer poses for a photograph. When his body was found after his famous Last Stand at the Battle of Little Bighorn, he had not been scalped—unlike many of his soldiers. The Sioux had not recognized him.

Chief Red Cloud leads an attack on Fort Phil Kearney. Captain Fetterman had taunted the Sioux by saying, "Give me 80 men and I shall ride through the whole Sioux nation." But when the Native Americans attacked, all his men were killed.

of woodcutters. When the army sent out its soldiers to defend the woodcutters, the Native Americans attacked them too. The army struck back. Red Cloud's War had begun. It lasted until April 1868, when the American government at last accepted defeat. The Native Americans burned down the fort. Red Cloud and the Sioux, the Arapahos, and the Cheyennes had won.

The last warriors

Red Cloud's victory at Fort Phil Kearney did not bring a bright future for the Native Americans. As white settlers continued to flood across their lands, many native peoples gave up and were forced onto reservations. By the 1880s, the Apaches were about the only threat left to the settlers.

The Apaches were fierce warriors who lived in the mountainous deserts of Arizona and New Mexico. They were divided into small tribes, which hardly ever agreed with one another. For years, the Apaches left the settlers alone, preferring to attack Mexicans. But in 1860, some Pinal Apaches attacked a settler's ranch and kidnaped a child.

This painting by the American artist Frederic Remington shows an Apache signaling the start of an ambush.

38

The boy's father reported the kidnaping to the army, and an officer named George Bascom was instructed to get the boy back. The blame had mistakenly been laid on

Cochise, the chief of the Chiricahua Apaches. Cochise, who knew nothing about the crime, was summoned to a meeting with Bascom.

Bascom was waiting for him in a tent close to a stagecoach station. The moment Cochise turned up, accompanied by five members of his family, they were all arrested. The furious chief used his knife to cut a hole in the tent where he was being held, and he managed to escape. But his companions were held hostage. So Cochise and his men ambushed a stagecoach and took some white people prisoner. All attempts to swap hostages failed, and the white prisoners were massacred by Cochise's men. Some of the Apache hostages were later hanged in revenge for these killings.

The incident made Cochise bitter. He and his warriors fought against the army for years, always resisting any attempts to force them into a reservation. They did not succeed. In April 1873, the last of the Apaches were sent off to the reservations, including the hated San Carlos reservation in Arizona. They were not treated well, and many ran away to their old homes. Cochise himself died in 1874.

A lone Native American is surrounded by a detachment of U.S. Cavalry officers. Life was often harsh for an army officer in the Wild West. He had to endure low wages, poor living conditions, and loneliness. If captured by hostile Native Americans, he risked a slow, horrible death. Many soldiers found the pressure too great and deserted.

Above The Apache chief Geronimo. In later life he became a Christian and joined the Dutch Reformed Church. In 1905, at Theodore Roosevelt's presidential inauguration, Geronimo joined in the festivities, traveling in an open car wearing a silk top hat. He died in 1909 at age 80.

Geronimo

In 1882, a band of Apaches led by a warrior named Goyathlay, who was called Geronimo by the Mexicans, escaped to Mexico. After being hunted by the army, they gave up and returned to the reservation. In 1885, Geronimo and a handful of other leaders escaped again, this time taking 140 Apaches with them. They fled to the Sierra Madre mountains. An army search party, led by General Crook, found the Apaches' hideout and destroyed it. Geronimo and the Apaches begged for a peace talk, but the general insisted that they should go to Florida. That night, someone sold whiskey to Geronimo and his followers. Geronimo and another chief, Nachez, got drunk and escaped once again, taking a small band of warriors, women, and children with them.

The army officers chased Geronimo around the Arizona desert. Eventually, the Apaches tired of life on the run, and

Above
Geronimo and his followers shortly after they had surrendered to General Crook in the Sierra Madre mountains in 1886.

Below A band of Apache prisoners at a rest stop on their way to exile in Florida, 1886

The Nez Percé

The persecution of the Nez Percé tribe was one of the greatest tragedies in the history of the Wild West. The Nez Percé were a peaceful people who had never killed a settler. They lived in the Wallowa Valley in Oregon and around the Salmon River in Idaho.

When settlers tried to claim the Wallowa Valley as their own, the Nez Percé chief, Joseph, refused to move to a reservation. The settlers were angry and the American army was ordered to move in. In 1877, Chief Joseph, fearing his people would be killed, started moving them out, but violence erupted between some of his men and a group of settlers. Joseph and his 750 tribe members fled eastward then up toward the Canadian border, where they planned to team up with exiled Sioux. The army pursued Chief Joseph's tribe relentlessly for three months, fighting fierce battles all the way. But the brave Nez Percé kept going for nearly 1,800 miles. When they finally surrendered, 120 people were dead. Another 300, including Chief Joseph's daughter, managed to join the Sioux in Canada, but the chief's wife had died.

As he handed in his guns and shook the army officer's hand, Chief Joseph made an eloquent speech, saying: "I am tired of fighting. It is cold and we have no blankets. The little children are freezing."

The Nez Percé were shipped to a reservation in Kansas, where many of them died. For years, Chief Joseph begged the authorities to let his people return to their lands. In 1885, they were allowed to go back to Washington state—but not to their beloved Wallowa Valley. Chief Joseph died in 1904.

When Chief Joseph died, it was said that he could not "accuse the United States of one single act of justice."

Geronimo and Nachez gave themselves up in 1886. They were sent to a jail in Florida, where most of them died. News of Geronimo's surrender shocked all the Native Americans. The Apaches had finally been subdued. By 1907, when Oklahoma was declared a state, the Native Americans' territory had disappeared altogether, apart from the reservations.

HOW THE WILD WEST WAS TAMED

Some people believe that the Wild West was officially tamed in 1893, when Fredrick Jackson Turner, a famous historian, declared the frontier officially closed. But things had started to change long before that.

The transcontinental railroad

During the 1840s, people talked of building a railroad line that connected the East with the West. Bickering over where the line should run held up the work for many years. But in 1862, it was decided that two companies—the Union Pacific and the Central Pacific—should

Many Chinese men were employed to work on the Central Pacific Railroad. Irishmen made up the workforce that built the Union Pacific line.

Under the terms of the Pacific Railway Acts of 1862–64, railroad companies were given permission to buy a wide belt of land along both sides of their routes. In all, they gained more than 205,000 square miles.

The first Union Pacific train chugs across the Western Plains toward the Pacific. The arrival of the railroad, called the iron horse by the Native Americans, speeded up the development of the American West.

undertake the job. The companies were given 37,500 square miles of public land for the job, and the work started in earnest in 1865. It was no small feat: About 1,800 miles of track had to be laid. The Union Pacific started laying lines westward from Omaha; the Central Pacific worked eastward. The two met at Promontory Point, Utah, on April 10, 1869. Nationwide celebrations followed. But the railroad lines put a stop to the big cattle trails. They also spelled disaster for the Native Americans, who were overwhelmed by the flood of white settlers on the lands alongside the railroad.

Fencing the West

Barbed wire was patented in 1873, and fencing was soon introduced to the open ranges of the West. At first, the big ranchers fought against it with all their power, but the idea caught on. After all, the fences created a clear mark between ranches and between

The introduction of barbed wire fences meant that cattle could no longer roam large areas and graze wherever they wanted. Cattlemen's disputes over land boundaries often became violent, and masked men sometimes cut down fences in protest. However, most ranchers discovered the benefits of fencing in their land and their herds.

grazing land and farmland. Fences also meant that thieves could not get to the cattle as easily as they had and that the cattle could not stray. The great days of open ranching were over.

Most cowboys looked down on the sheepmen and hated the sheep that, they claimed, ate too much grass. They thought nothing of shooting a sheepman. As the cattle trade changed, however, many cowboys became sheepmen themselves.

The end of the cowboys

At the same time, many ranchers built windmills, which helped to pump water straight onto their lands. More cattle could now be raised in one place. All this meant that fewer cowboys were needed to look after the herds. Many lost their jobs.

During the winter of 1885–86, blizzards and wild storms wiped out many cattle herds in the West. Hundreds of cowboys died trying to save them, and many big cattle ranchers went out of business. Others gave up open ranching in favor of small, efficient farms. The cowboys found that they had to do much more than look after the herds. To their disgust, they had to do farm jobs on foot, and the ranchers insisted that they should collect hay in case another freezing winter came.

Many cowboys turned to other occupations—even

CANADA

PACIFIC OCEAN

MEXICO

GULF OF MEXICO

the hated job of sheep tending. Sheep rearing and farming had always been frowned on by ranchers and cowboys, but the farmers and the sheepmen now won more control over the land.

Many cowboys were left jobless and bitter. They saw the farmers as destroyers of the open ranges. With the Native Americans consigned to reservations and many towns cleaned up for new settlers, the Wild West had finally been tamed forever.

Below The Wild Bunch in 1910: They were a gang of infamous outlaws led by Robert L. Parker (alias Butch Cassidy, bottom right) and Harry Longbaugh (the "Sundance Kid," bottom left). For years, they robbed trains, but by the end of the 1890s the risk of being caught was too great, and Butch and Sundance fled to South America.

Above Chief Sitting Bull of the Teton Sioux believed that the West would be the Native Americans' country again. His dream never came true, and he died fighting for his people in 1890. That same year, the Native Americans suffered their final defeat at the Battle of Wounded Knee. By 1894, they had all been forced onto reservations dotted around the United States.

TIME LINE

A.D. 1850	1870	1890

1775–83
●
American Revolution

1811
●
First steamboat from New Orleans sails up Mississippi

1832
●
The U.S. government declares that all land west of the Mississippi is Native American territory

1842
●
Oregon Trail begins

1847
●
Mormons settle in Utah

1848
●
Gold found in California. Start of Gold Rush

1858
●
Start of Butterfield stagecoach line

1860–65
●
Civil War

1862
●
Homestead Act gives farmers large plots of land to turn into farms

1866
●
Chief Red Cloud and the Sioux attack Fort Phil Kearney. Jesse James and his gang rob bank in Liberty

1867
●
Start of the great cattle drives to Abilene, Kansas

1868
●
End of Red Cloud's War

1869
●
Railroad lines join East and West coasts

1874
●
Chief Cochise dies

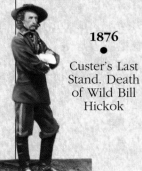

1876
●
Custer's Last Stand. Death of Wild Bill Hickok

1877
●
Chief Joseph surrenders

1881
●
Wyatt Earp wins gunfight at O.K. Corral. Pat Garrett kills Billy the Kid

1882
●
Jesse James murdered by a gang member. Geronimo escapes from a reservation

1883
●
Buffalo Bill starts his Wild West Show

1886
●
Geronimo surrenders

1890
●
Final defeat of Native Americans at Battle of Wounded Knee. Frontier declared officially closed in 1893

1904
●
Death of Chief Joseph of the Nez Percé

1907
●
The last tract of Native American territory in Kansas disappears

1909
●
Death of Geronimo and Red Cloud

46

GLOSSARY

Emigrate To leave your own country and go to live in another.

Gopher A small animal that lives in burrows under the ground.

Pioneers The first people to explore or settle in a new land.

Rancher A person who owns or works on a ranch where livestock—especially cattle—are raised.

Reservation An area of land where Native Americans were forced to live after their own lands had been taken from them.

Spur A small metal wheel with spikes fixed to the heel of a cowboy's riding boot and used for urging on his horse.

Trading posts The first general stores or shops set up in the frontier lands for the pioneers and Native Americans.

Vigilante A member of a group that attempts to keep law and order and punish lawbreakers without the authority of the government and the law courts.

FURTHER INFORMATION

MOVIES

The Alamo (1960) The heroic fight between the Texans and the Mexicans.

Broken Lance (1954) A powerful drama set on the high range in the 1890s. Ranchers clash with miners and family members plot to take over the ranch.

Dances with Wolves (1990) Kevin Costner stars as an army lieutenant who opts to live with Native Americans.

How the West Was Won (1962) A film that depicts the entire story of the Wild West.

Indians of North America Video Collection. A 10-video series on the history of various Native American peoples. Produced by Chelsea House publishers.

Red River (1948) An exciting film that shows what life was like on the great cattle trail.

Stagecoach (1939) A famous film featuring an Apache attack on a stagecoach and Geronimo, the Native American chief.

CD-Rom

The American Indian: A Multimedia Encyclopedia. New York: Facts on File, 1993.

BOOKS

Bentley, Judith. *Brides, Midwives, and Widows*. Settling the West. New York: 21st Century Books, 1995.

Collins, James L. *Settling the American West*. First Books. New York: Franklin Watts, 1993.

DiCerto, Joseph J. *The Pony Express: Hoofbeats in the Wilderness*. First Books. New York: Franklin Watts, 1989.

Hicks, Peter. *The Sioux*. Look into the Past. New York: Thomson Learning, 1994.

Nardo, Don. *The Indian Wars*. America's Wars. San Diego: Lucent Books, 1991.

Ross, Stewart. *Cowboys*. Fact or Fiction. Brookfield, CT: Copper Beech, 1995.

Smith, Carter, ed. *The Legendary Wild West*. American Albums from the Collection of the Library of Congress. Brookfield, CT: Millbrook Press, 1992.

Steele, Philip. *Little Bighorn*. Great Battles and Sieges. New York: New Discovery, 1992.

Winslow, Mimi. *Loggers and Railroad Workers*. Settling the West. New York: 21st Century Books, 1995.

INDEX